GOES-U LAUNCH

Everything you need to know about the fourth and final satellite in the (GOES) — R Series

Charles D. Battle

Intentionally left blank

GOES-U Launch

Everything you need to know about the fourth and final satellite in the (GOES) – R Series.

By

Charles D. Battle

Gratitude

Dear reader, I want to give special thanks to you for your efforts and concerns towards educating yourself. I want to thank you for choosing my book among other books.

We have put in so much effort so that this book will satisfy your interest in knowing more about GOES-U (the fourth and the final satellite in the GOES–R Series). Join us today to know everything about the GOES-U Mission.

Intentionally left blank

Table Of Contents

Introduction..8

Chapter 1: The GOES-U Launch......................12

Pre-Launch Preparations..................................... 12

The Launch Event... 14

Post-Launch Analysis....................................15

Chapter 2: GOES-U Mission Overview..............18

The GOES-R Series: A Legacy of Innovation in Weather Observation.. 18

GOES-U Preview..20

The Renaming to GOES-19................................ 22

The Role of GOES-19 in the GOES East and West Operations.. 24

Chapter 3: Monitoring Weather and Environmental Phenomena on Earth.................. 28

The Advanced Baseline Imager (ABI)...............28

The Geostationary Lightning Mapper (GLM).. 32

The Importance of International Collaboration in Weather Monitoring... 35

Chapter 4: Monitoring the Sun and Space Weather..38

Introduction to Space Weather Monitoring.......38

The Extreme Ultraviolet and X-ray Irradiance Sensors (EXIS) and Solar Ultraviolet Imager (SUVI)..39

The Compact Coronagraph-1 (CCOR-1): A New Addition...42

The Magnetometer and Space Environment In-Situ Suite (SEISS)............................... 44

Implications of Space Weather Forecasts..........46

Chapter 5: Benefits of the GOES-U Mission......50

Chapter 6: Legacy of GOES-U.............................60

Building Upon a Strong Foundation of Past Missions... 60

A Stepping Stone for Future Advancements in Weather and Environmental Observation......... 62

Conclusion.. 64

Introduction

Brief Overview of the Book.

Welcome, intrepid reader, to the captivating realm of space exploration! This book, titled "GOES-U Launch: Everything You Need to Know About the Fourth and Final Satellite in the (GOES) – R Series," serves as your passport to a celestial adventure. This comprehensive guide unveils the intricacies of the GOES-U mission, the crowning achievement of the Geostationary Operational Environmental Satellites (GOES) – R Series. We'll embark on a careful exploration, dissecting the mission's objectives, the innovative technology that brings it to life, and the transformative impact it will have on the way we observe and understand weather patterns and environmental phenomena. From its inception, fueled by the ingenuity of human minds, to its anticipated contributions to the vast landscape of science and technology, this book leaves no stone unturned. Whether you're a seasoned space aficionado or a curious newcomer eager to unravel the mysteries of the cosmos, this book is designed to be your trusty companion.

Importance of Space Missions.

Space missions transcend the realm of mere celestial exploration; they represent a pivotal undertaking for humanity. They serve as our eyes and ears in the vast cosmic ocean, aiding us in comprehending the universe that surrounds us. Through these audacious endeavors, we seek answers to fundamental questions that have captivated humankind for millennia: Where do we come from? What is the origin of the universe? Are we truly alone in this vast expanse?

The pursuit of knowledge isn't the sole benefit gleaned from space exploration. These missions have demonstrably practical applications, fostering advancements in technology that ripple through our everyday lives. From the creation of life-saving medical devices to the development of revolutionary communication systems, space exploration acts as a catalyst for innovation, propelling our technological prowess forward.

Furthermore, space missions serve as an economic powerhouse, creating lucrative jobs in cutting-edge fields and stimulating growth across various sectors. They inspire a new generation of scientists, engineers, and dreamers, paving the way for a brighter future brimming with groundbreaking discoveries.

However, the impact of space missions extends far beyond technological marvels and economic gains. Missions like GOES-U play a critical role in safeguarding our planet. By carefully monitoring Earth's weather patterns, oceans, and environment, GOES-U will provide us with invaluable data, enabling us to detect and monitor environmental phenomena with unprecedented precision. This information is the cornerstone for accurate weather forecasting, allowing us to track potentially devastating storms and prepare for their impact. Additionally, it offers crucial insights into the ever-evolving phenomenon of climate change, empowering us to make informed decisions for a sustainable future.

In essence, space missions are not just about venturing into the unknown; they are about safeguarding our home planet, Earth, and fostering a deeper understanding of the intricate systems that sustain life as we know it.

Intentionally left blank

Chapter 1: The GOES-U Launch

Pre-Launch Preparations

The odyssey of the GOES-U satellite commences not amidst the celestial expanse, but within the confines of Lockheed Martin Space's facility in Littleton, Colorado. Here, careful minds and steady hands bring the marvel of technology to life. Over a span of years, the GOES-U team carefully constructs the instruments and spacecraft, carefully integrating each intricate component. But this intricate dance isn't solely about assembly; it's a rigorous waltz with quality assurance. The satellite undergoes a battery of tests, simulating the unforgiving environment of launch and ensuring its functionality upon reaching its designated geostationary orbit, a staggering 22,236 miles above Earth's surface.

Once the construction and testing phases are complete, GOES-U embarks on its next leg of the journey. However, transporting a technological marvel the size of a small school bus, weighing over 6,000 pounds, is no easy feat. Imagine the logistical ballet involved! GOES-U is carefully secured and carefully shipped from the familiar Colorado landscape to the sun-drenched Kennedy Space Center in Florida.

Upon arrival in Florida, GOES-U is transported to Astrotech Space Operations in nearby Titusville. Here, a new chapter unfolds, focusing on cautious verification. The satellite undergoes a comprehensive series of electrical tests, ensuring its internal systems are functioning flawlessly. Mechanical configurations are also carefully reviewed and adjusted to prepare GOES-U for the momentous launch.

One of the most critical pre-launch preparations involves fueling the satellite. Propelling GOES-U to its designated orbit and sustaining its operations for a remarkable 15 years demands a substantial amount of propellant – a staggering total exceeding 5,000 pounds of fuel and oxidizer! This cautious fueling process ensures GOES-U has the necessary resources to fulfill its mission for over a decade.

The Launch Event

The launch of the GOES-U mission is targeted for around the earlier month of June. The chosen launch vehicle for this momentous occasion is no less impressive – the mighty **Falcon Heavy rocket**, a leviathan of the skies crafted by SpaceX. This marks a historic first for the GOES program, signifying a new era of collaboration and technological advancement. The estimated cost for NASA to entrust SpaceX with this critical mission is approximately $152.5 million.

The launch itself will be spectacle unlike any other. The immense power of the Falcon Heavy rocket will propel GOES-U skyward, leaving a trail of fire and smoke as it breaks free from Earth's atmosphere. The ground will tremble with the sheer force of the launch, a testament to the immense power required to overcome Earth's gravitational pull. As the rocket ascends, individuals will witness a breathtaking display of human ingenuity and technological prowess.

Post-Launch Analysis

Following the successful launch of GOES-U, a period of careful post-launch testing ensues. This critical phase serves to validate the functionality of both the satellite itself and the ground systems that will communicate with and receive data from GOES-U. The success of the mission hinges on this rigorous testing process.

One of the most crucial aspects of post-launch analysis involves ensuring the proper deployment of the satellite's expansive five-panel solar array. Folded compactly during launch for optimal space utilization, this immense structure will unfurl upon reaching geostationary orbit. The successful deployment of this solar array is paramount, as the photovoltaic cells embedded within will convert the sun's energy into electricity, powering the entire satellite – its instruments, computers, data processors, sensors, and telecommunication equipment. Without this vital source of energy, GOES-U would be rendered inoperable.

The post-launch analysis also encompasses a comprehensive evaluation of the satellite's instruments. These instruments, the heart and soul of the GOES-U mission, are designed to collect a vast array of critical data – atmospheric conditions, hydrological patterns, oceanic characteristics, climatic trends, solar activity, and space weather phenomena. Rigorous testing ensures these instruments are functioning optimally, ready to deliver the data that will revolutionize our understanding of Earth and its surrounding environment.

The success of each phase is crucial for the overall mission, paving the way for GOES-U to fulfill its critical role in safeguarding our planet and furthering our understanding of the universe.

Intentionally left blank

Chapter 2: GOES-U Mission Overview

The GOES-R Series: A Legacy of Innovation in Weather Observation.

The GOES-R Series represents a monumental leap forward in NOAA's arsenal of Geostationary Operational Environmental Satellites (GOES). This state-of-the-art constellation stands as the most advanced geostationary weather observation system ever deployed for the nation. The GOES-R Series signifies a commitment to continuous improvement, ensuring the United States remains at the forefront of weather monitoring and environmental data collection.

The series itself comprises four carefully crafted satellites: GOES-R, GOES-S, GOES-T, and the soon-to-be-launched GOES-U. These marvels of engineering possess a unique orbital characteristic – they traverse Earth's equatorial plane at a velocity precisely matching the planet's rotation. This remarkable feat allows them to maintain a fixed position relative to Earth, a concept known as geostationary orbit. By remaining stationary in the sky, these satellites can provide continuous, uninterrupted observation of a specific region, offering invaluable insights into weather patterns, environmental changes, and space weather phenomena.

The GOES-R Series isn't merely about maintaining a fixed gaze; it's about revolutionizing the way we observe and understand our planet. These satellites boast an impressive array of capabilities. They capture advanced imagery, carefully measuring atmospheric conditions across vast stretches of the globe. Additionally, they gather intricate atmospheric measurements, providing a deeper understanding of the complex systems that govern weather patterns. But the advancements extend beyond atmospheric observation. The GOES-R Series incorporates real-time mapping of total lightning activity, offering crucial insights into the development and movement of potentially destructive storms. This capability empowers meteorologists to issue timely warnings and safeguard communities from the wrath of nature.

Perhaps one of the most significant contributions of the GOES-R Series lies in its enhanced monitoring of solar activity and space weather. Our Sun, a celestial powerhouse, is not a constant entity. It undergoes periods of intense activity, releasing bursts of charged particles and radiation that can disrupt satellites, communication systems, and power grids. The GOES-R Series acts as our vigilant eye in the sky, carefully monitoring these solar outbursts and providing critical early warnings, allowing us to mitigate their potential impact.

In addition, the GOES-R Series is a testament to human ingenuity and a cornerstone of modern weather observation. It has transformed our ability to predict and prepare for weather events, fostered a deeper understanding of space weather, and safeguarded our infrastructure from the capricious nature of the Sun. The launch of GOES-U signifies the culmination of years of careful planning and technological advancements, further solidifying the GOES-R Series' legacy as a vital tool for environmental monitoring and weather forecasting.

GOES-U Preview

GOES-U stands as the crowning achievement of the GOES-R Series, the fourth and final satellite carefully crafted to revolutionize our understanding of Earth and its surrounding environment. Its integration into the constellation signifies a new era of environmental monitoring capabilities, further solidifying the GOES-R Series' position as the Western Hemisphere's most sophisticated weather observation and environmental monitoring system.

Similar to its predecessors, GOES-U boasts a suite of advanced instruments designed to capture a comprehensive picture of Earth's ever-changing dynamics. These instruments gather invaluable data on atmospheric conditions, providing meteorologists with a deeper understanding of the forces shaping weather patterns. GOES-U's advanced imaging capabilities allow for the creation of detailed, real-time visualizations of weather systems, empowering forecasters to issue more accurate and timely weather warnings.

But GOES-U's contributions extend beyond traditional weather observation. The satellite incorporates cutting-edge technology specifically designed to monitor lightning activity in real-time. This capability offers crucial insights into the development and movement of potentially destructive storms, allowing for improved preparedness and mitigation efforts. Furthermore,

GOES-U plays a vital role in safeguarding our technology from the unpredictable nature of space weather. By carefully monitoring solar activity and the emission of charged particles, GOES-U provides early warnings of potential disruptions to satellites, communication systems, and power grids. This advanced space weather monitoring capability is a cornerstone of safeguarding critical infrastructure and ensuring the smooth operation of communication networks.

GOES-U represents the culmination of cutting-edge technology and careful planning. Its integration into the GOES-R Series signifies a significant leap forward in our ability to observe and understand Earth's complex environmental systems. The data collected by GOES-U will empower meteorologists to provide more accurate forecasts, safeguard communities from extreme weather events, and protect our infrastructure from the potential disruption of space weather.

The Renaming to GOES-19

The GOES-U nickname serves the satellite valiantly throughout its ground testing and launch phases.

However, upon reaching its designated geostationary orbit, GOES-U undergoes a symbolic transformation – it is renamed as GOES-19. This seemingly simple act of renaming holds a deeper significance within the GOES program.

The GOES program adheres to a sequential naming convention. Each operational GOES satellite receives a numerical designation reflecting its order of launch within the series. GOES-16, currently occupying the GOES-East position, exemplifies this convention. GOES-U, slated to replace GOES-16, inherits the subsequent number in the sequence, thus becoming GOES-19.

This transformation from GOES-U to GOES-19 signifies not just a change in name, but a transition to operational status. GOES-19 will join the ranks of its predecessors, actively collecting and transmitting critical environmental data. This data will be disseminated to weather forecasting agencies across the globe, empowering meteorologists to make informed predictions and issue timely warnings.

The journey from GOES-U to GOES-19 embodies the culmination of years of careful planning, engineering, and testing. It represents the transformation of a technological marvel from a grounded prototype to a vital component of the

GOES constellation, actively safeguarding our planet and furthering our understanding of Earth's intricate environmental systems.

The Role of GOES-19 in the GOES East and West Operations

Following a rigorous on-orbit checkout process, carefully verifying the functionality of its instruments and systems, GOES-19 will be integrated into NOAA's operational GOES constellation. This signifies a pivotal moment, as GOES-19 is poised to assume a critical role within the GOES East and West operational framework.

NOAA strategically positions two operational GOES satellites in geostationary orbit, each designated for a specific region: GOES-East and GOES-West. GOES-16 currently occupies the GOES-East position, providing continuous observation of weather patterns and environmental conditions across the Eastern Hemisphere and western Atlantic Ocean. Upon assuming operational status, GOES-19 is slated to replace GOES-16, becoming the vigilant eye in the sky for the GOES-East sector.

GOES-18, GOES-19's soon-to-be partner, currently reigns supreme in the GOES-West domain. This dynamic duo, GOES-19 (GOES-East) and GOES-18 (GOES-West), will work in harmonious synergy, providing comprehensive coverage of a vast expanse – stretching from the west coast of Africa to the far reaches of New Zealand.

The collaborative efforts of GOES-19 and GOES-18 offer a multitude of benefits. The combined data collected by these two satellites paints a more complete picture of global weather patterns, fostering a deeper understanding of atmospheric dynamics and climatic trends. This comprehensive data set empowers meteorologists to issue more accurate and timely weather forecasts, potentially saving lives and mitigating the impact of severe weather events.

Furthermore, the combined monitoring capabilities of GOES-19 and GOES-18 bolster our preparedness for space weather occurrences. By carefully observing solar activity from two vantage points, these satellites offer a more comprehensive view of potential solar flares and coronal mass ejections. This enhanced monitoring capability allows for the issuance of more precise and timely warnings, safeguarding critical infrastructure from the disruptive effects of space weather.

In conclusion, the GOES-U mission, culminating in the operational status of GOES-19, signifies a significant leap forward in our ability to monitor Earth's weather patterns, environmental conditions, and space weather phenomena. GOES-19's integration into the GOES East and West operational framework, working in hand with GOES-18, strengthens our observational capabilities and fosters a deeper understanding of the complex systems governing our planet. This collaborative effort empowers us to make informed decisions, safeguard our communities, and navigate the ever-changing dynamics of our environment.

Intentionally left blank

Chapter 3: Monitoring Weather and Environmental Phenomena on Earth

The Advanced Baseline Imager (ABI)

An Overview:

The Advanced Baseline Imager (ABI) stands as the crown jewel of the GOES-R Series, serving as the primary instrument for carefully capturing images of Earth's weather patterns, oceans, and environment. Functioning similarly to a human eye, the ABI offers an unparalleled view of our planet, carefully dissecting its ever-changing dynamics.

One of the defining characteristics of the ABI is its exceptional spectral range. Unlike its predecessors, the ABI observes Earth through 16 distinct spectral bands. Imagine these bands as different colored filters, each revealing a unique aspect of our planet. Two of these bands fall within the visible spectrum, allowing the ABI to capture images closely resembling what the human eye perceives. However, the true power lies in the remaining fourteen bands, venturing beyond the realm of human vision and into the realm of the infrared and near-infrared. These intricate spectral bands serve as powerful tools for scientists and meteorologists, allowing them to identify and differentiate various elements on Earth's surface and within the atmosphere. For instance, by analyzing specific bands, scientists can distinguish between the lush greenery of forests, the vast expanse of oceans, the wispy trails of clouds, the invisible presence of atmospheric moisture, or the ominous plumes of smoke rising from a wildfire. The capabilities of the ABI extend far beyond mere observation; it represents a significant step in environmental data collection. Compared to its predecessors, the ABI boasts a staggering increase in the amount of spectral information it gathers – a remarkable three times more than previous systems. This translates to a more comprehensive picture of Earth's intricate environmental tapestry.

Furthermore, the ABI offers a fourfold improvement in spatial resolution. Imagine the difference between a blurry photograph and a high-definition image; the ABI delivers the latter, allowing for a much clearer and more detailed analysis of weather patterns, environmental phenomena, and potential hazards. The final piece of the puzzle lies in temporal coverage. The ABI captures images at a rate exceeding five times faster than previous systems. This translates to near-real-time monitoring, empowering meteorologists to track rapidly developing weather systems and anticipate potential threats with unprecedented accuracy.

The ABI represents a paradigm shift in our ability to observe and understand Earth. Its exceptional spectral range, enhanced spatial resolution, and rapid temporal coverage unlock a treasure trove of environmental data, empowering us to make informed decisions.

Applications of ABI Data.

The data gleaned from the ABI isn't confined to a single domain; it has a far-reaching impact across a diverse spectrum of environmental applications. Meteorologists leverage this invaluable data to carefully track and monitor the formation and movement of clouds, a crucial aspect of weather forecasting. By analyzing ABI data, they can decipher atmospheric motion, a key factor in understanding and predicting weather patterns.

Furthermore, the ABI offers insights into the phenomenon of convection, the vertical movement of air within the atmosphere, which plays a significant role in the development of storms.

Beyond weather forecasting, ABI data empowers scientists to monitor land surface temperatures, a critical factor in understanding climate change and its impact on ecosystems.

Additionally, the ABI sheds light on the dynamic nature of our oceans, revealing vital information about water circulation patterns and ocean health. The data can also be harnessed to track the flow of water across landscapes, providing insights into flood risks and water resource management.

The applications of ABI data extend beyond natural phenomena. It serves as a powerful tool for monitoring wildfires and the smoke plumes they generate, allowing for improved response efforts and mitigation strategies. Similarly, the ABI can detect volcanic ash plumes, empowering authorities to issue timely warnings and safeguard communities from the potential dangers of volcanic eruptions. ABI data also plays a vital role in monitoring air quality by detecting the presence of aerosols, tiny particles suspended in the atmosphere that can have a significant impact on human health. Finally, the

ABI offers a unique perspective on the health of vegetation, allowing scientists to monitor changes in plant life and identify potential environmental threats.

To sum it up, ABI data serves as a versatile tool for environmental monitoring, encompassing a wide range of applications across weather forecasting, oceanography, land management, disaster mitigation, air quality monitoring, and vegetation health assessment.

The Geostationary Lightning Mapper (GLM)

An Overview:

While the ABI offers a detailed visual depiction of Earth's ever-changing tapestry, the Geostationary Lightning Mapper (GLM) delves deeper, unveiling the unseen electrical fury lurking within the atmosphere. Functioning as a dedicated lightning detection instrument, the GLM represents a revolutionary advancement in our ability to monitor and understand this powerful natural phenomenon.

The GLM boasts a unique design – a single-channel, near-infrared optical transient detector carefully positioned on the GOES-16 satellite within geostationary orbit. This strategic placement offers a distinct advantage. Unlike traditional ground-based lightning detection networks, the GLM enjoys a continuous view of a designated region, encompassing the United States. This translates to unparalleled lightning detection capabilities, offering a rate of observation far exceeding anything previously achievable from space.

One of the most significant strengths of the GLM lies in its ability to detect all forms of lightning – cloud-to-cloud, cloud-to-ground, and intra-cloud flashes – with exceptional efficiency. Furthermore, unlike ground-based networks that are rendered ineffective during night-time hours, the GLM operates continuously, providing 24/7 lightning detection capabilities. This continuous monitoring is particularly crucial, as lightning activity can often serve as a precursor to severe weather events.

The GLM doesn't merely detect lightning; it does so with remarkable precision. The instrument boasts high spatial resolution, allowing for the pinpointing of lightning strikes with exceptional accuracy.

Role of GLM in Weather Forecasting.

The data gleaned from the GLM isn't merely a scientific curiosity; it holds immense practical value, particularly in the realm of weather forecasting. Prior to the advent of the GLM, meteorologists relied primarily on radar data to identify and predict severe storms. While radar offers valuable insights, it has limitations. It can only detect the presence of precipitation, not the electrical activity within a storm that often precedes the formation of rain or hail.

The GLM bridges this critical gap in weather observation. By detecting lightning activity, the GLM offers a glimpse into the inner workings of a storm, revealing the presence of vigorous atmospheric convection – a key ingredient for the development of severe weather events such as tornadoes, hailstorms, and damaging winds. This early warning capability empowers meteorologists to issue more timely and accurate severe weather warnings, potentially saving lives and safeguarding communities from harm.

For instance, studies have shown that a rapid increase in lightning activity within a storm system can be a strong indicator of an impending tornado. The GLM, with its ability to detect and monitor lightning in near-real time, allows meteorologists to identify such rapid increases and issue timely tornado warnings, providing precious lead time for communities to take shelter.

The Importance of International Collaboration in Weather Monitoring.

The Earth's atmosphere transcends political boundaries. Weather systems don't adhere to national borders; they traverse continents and oceans, impacting the lives of people across the globe. Therefore, international collaboration in weather monitoring is not merely a diplomatic nicety; it's a necessity for effective weather forecasting and risk management.

Meteorologists depends on observations across the entire globe and near-instantaneous exchange of weather information. Imagine a meteorologist in the United States attempting to forecast a weather system that originated in Africa; without access to real-time data on the storm's development and movement, their predictions would be similar to educated guesses. International collaboration bridges this gap, fostering the seamless exchange of weather data between nations. This allows meteorologists to have a more comprehensive picture of global weather patterns, leading to more accurate forecasts for all.

Beyond the immediate benefits of improved weather forecasting, international collaboration is crucial for managing the impacts of climate change, a global phenomenon with far-reaching consequences. By sharing environmental observation data, nations can gain a deeper understanding of how climate change is manifesting itself in different regions of the world. This shared knowledge empowers nations to develop more effective strategies for mitigating the effects of climate change and adapting to its inevitable consequences. For instance, by sharing data on rising sea levels or changes in precipitation patterns, nations can work together to implement coastal protection measures and develop sustainable water management practices.

International collaboration in weather monitoring extends beyond data exchange. It fosters a spirit of scientific cooperation, allowing researchers from different nations to share their expertise and work together on developing new technologies and methodologies for weather observation and environmental monitoring. This collaborative approach accelerates advancements in the field, ultimately leading to a more comprehensive understanding of our planet's complex atmospheric and environmental systems.

Furthermore, international collaboration fosters a sense of global responsibility for weather preparedness and disaster risk reduction. By sharing resources and expertise, nations can better assist each other in preparing for and responding to natural disasters. For instance, a nation with advanced satellite technology can share data with a less developed nation facing an impending storm, enabling them to issue timely warnings and evacuate vulnerable populations.

Chapter 4: Monitoring the Sun and Space Weather

Introduction to Space Weather Monitoring

While our focus often lies on the ever-changing dynamics of Earth's weather patterns, a potent force lurks beyond our atmosphere – the Sun. This celestial powerhouse isn't a constant entity; it undergoes periods of intense activity, releasing bursts of charged particles and radiation that can disrupt our way of life. This realm of solar activity and its impact on Earth's environment is known as space weather.

Space weather monitoring plays a vital role in safeguarding our planet and its inhabitants from the Sun's unpredictable outbursts. This specialized discipline aims to understand the complex processes governing solar activity, predict the resulting disturbances in the space environment, and forecast their potential impact on Earth's infrastructure and human life. The effects of space weather can range from subtle to catastrophic. On one end of the spectrum, charged particles from the Sun can damage sensitive electronics aboard satellites, disrupting communication networks. At the other extreme, powerful solar storms can trigger geomagnetic disturbances on Earth, leading to widespread power grid outrages and infrastructure damage.

Understanding and predicting space weather is allied to deciphering the whispers and shouts of a distant giant. Fortunately, we aren't powerless in the face of the Sun's fury. By carefully monitoring solar activity and the resulting space environment, we can anticipate potential threats and take necessary precautions to mitigate their impact. The GOES-R Series, with its suite of advanced instruments, stands as a sentinel at the forefront of space weather monitoring.

The Extreme Ultraviolet and X-ray Irradiance Sensors (EXIS) and Solar Ultraviolet Imager (SUVI)

The GOES-R Series boasts a powerful pair for monitoring the Sun's activity – the **Solar Ultraviolet**

Imager (SUVI) and the **Extreme Ultraviolet and X-ray Irradiance Sensors (EXIS).** These instruments function as the eyes of the GOES satellites, carefully dissecting the Sun's ever-changing state.

SUVI operates within the ultraviolet spectrum, invisible to the human eye. However, this seemingly obscure realm offers invaluable insights into the Sun's behavior. By capturing images in various ultraviolet wavelengths, SUVI allows scientists to observe the Sun's chromosphere and transition region – the turbulent layers of the Sun's atmosphere where solar flares erupt. These observations empower them to identify potential flare activity and predict their intensity. Furthermore, SUVI monitors solar features like coronal holes – regions of the Sun's corona with cooler temperatures and lower densities. Coronal holes play a significant role in the solar wind, a stream of charged particles constantly emanating from the Sun. By monitoring these features, SUVI aids in understanding and predicting fluctuations in the solar wind, which can impact Earth's magnetosphere.

EXIS complements SUVI by venturing even further into the realm of invisible light – the extreme ultraviolet and X-ray spectrum. These high-energy wavelengths are emitted by the Sun's corona during periods of intense activity, such as solar flares. EXIS carefully measures the intensity of this radiation, providing crucial data for assessing potential hazards. This information is vital for safeguarding astronauts and satellites from the harmful effects of solar radiation exposure. Additionally, EXIS data plays a pivotal role in monitoring the impact of solar activity on radio communication. During periods of intense solar flares, the increased level of X-ray radiation can disrupt radio signals, potentially hindering communication networks. By providing early warnings of such events, EXIS empowers communication providers to take necessary steps to mitigate these disruptions.

To conclude with, SUVI and EXIS act as a dynamic pair, offering a comprehensive view of the Sun's activity. The data gleaned from these instruments empowers us to understand the Sun's behavior, predict potential space weather threats, and safeguard our infrastructure and technology from their disruptive effects.

The Compact Coronagraph-1 (CCOR-1): A New Addition

The GOES-R Series is a testament to continuous improvement, and the GOES-U mission signifies the integration of a groundbreaking new instrument – the Compact Coronagraph-1 (CCOR-1). Unlike its predecessors, GOES-U boasts this innovative instrument specifically designed to unveil the secrets of the Sun's corona, the outermost layer of its atmosphere.

The corona is a region of extreme temperatures and tenuous plasma, often shrouded in mystery due to its faintness compared to the Sun's brilliant surface. However, the corona plays a pivotal role in space weather, as it's the birthplace of a celestial phenomenon known as a Coronal Mass Ejection (CME). CMEs are massive eruptions of superheated plasma and magnetic field lines that can hurtle towards Earth at incredible speeds. These potent outbursts can trigger geomagnetic storms upon reaching Earth's magnetosphere, potentially disrupting power grids and communication networks.

CCOR-1 addresses this challenge by functioning as a specialized telescope, employing a technique known as coronagraphy. In essence, the coronagraph blocks out the Sun's blinding light, allowing CCOR-1 to capture detailed images of the faint corona. These images provide invaluable insights into the development and characteristics of CMEs. CCOR-1 doesn't merely capture a single snapshot; it operates continuously, acquiring a sequence of CME images. By analyzing these sequences, scientists can determine crucial parameters of a CME, such as its size, velocity, and density. This information is paramount for predicting the potential impact of a CME on Earth's magnetosphere and issuing timely warnings if necessary.

The inclusion of CCOR-1 in the GOES-U mission marks a step forward in our ability to monitor and understand CMEs. The detailed data it gathers empowers us to anticipate potential geomagnetic storms with greater accuracy, safeguarding critical infrastructure and enabling us to take proactive measures to mitigate the disruptive effects of space weather.

The Magnetometer and Space Environment In-Situ Suite (SEISS)

The Magnetometer on the GOES-R Series doesn't rely on capturing images; instead, it functions as a highly sensitive compass, carefully measuring the strength and direction of Earth's magnetic field at the satellite's location. Imagine the Magnetometer as a sophisticated sensor array constantly gauging the ever-changing nature of this invisible force field. Earth's magnetic field isn't static; it's a dynamic entity, constantly buffeted by the solar wind and the internal workings of our planet's core. The Magnetometer plays a critical role in monitoring these fluctuations, offering invaluable insights into the health and responsiveness of Earth's magnetic shield. It also helps in:-

-Mapping the Magnetic Field Lines

-Monitoring Geomagnetic Storms:

-Understanding Magnetospheric Processes:

SEISS and the Magnetometer, while functioning as distinct instruments, offer a powerful synergy when their data is analyzed together. Imagine having one hand focused on the actors (energetic particles) and the other on the stage (magnetic field). By combining the information on the particle population from SEISS with the magnetic field data from the Magnetometer, scientists can paint a far more comprehensive picture of what's transpiring within the space environment.

Take for example, a sudden increase in energetic particle flux detected by SEISS, coupled with a corresponding fluctuation in the magnetic field measured by the Magnetometer, can provide a strong indication of a CME interacting with Earth's magnetosphere. This combined knowledge empowers scientists to not only forecast the arrival of a geomagnetic storm but also anticipate its potential intensity and impact.

In conclusion, SEISS and the Magnetometer represent a powerful twosome within the GOES-R Series. SEISS, with its suite of particle sensors, unveils the invisible population of energetic particles, while the Magnetometer carefully tracks the ever-changing nature of Earth's magnetic field. As they work hand-in-hand, these instruments offer a systemic perspective on the space environment, empowering us to safeguard our planet from the

Sun's fury and navigate the dynamic realm of space weather.

Implications of Space Weather Forecasts

Just as weather forecasts empower us to prepare for thunderstorms or blizzards, space weather forecasts offer a vital tool for mitigating the disruptions caused by the Sun's activity. The potential consequences of severe space weather events can be significant, impacting a wide range of technological infrastructure and even human health.

- One of the most critical implications of space weather forecasts lies in safeguarding our power grids. During geomagnetic storms triggered by CMEs, powerful currents are induced within the Earth's magnetosphere. These currents can surge through power grids, overloading transformers and causing widespread blackouts. Accurate space weather forecasts allow power grid operators to take necessary precautions, such as strategically rerouting power or implementing transformer protection measures. By anticipating potential geomagnetic storms, these proactive steps can minimize the risk of widespread power outages and safeguard critical infrastructure.

- Another crucial implication of space weather forecasts pertains to satellite communication. The same energetic particles responsible for geomagnetic storms can also disrupt radio signals, hindering communication between satellites and ground stations. Space weather forecasts empower satellite operators to take mitigating actions, such as temporarily switching to alternative communication channels or placing satellites in a safe mode. This foreknowledge safeguards critical communication infrastructure, ensuring the uninterrupted flow of data and information.

- Beyond infrastructure concerns, space weather forecasts also play a vital role in protecting human health. Astronauts venturing beyond Earth's protective magnetosphere are exposed to the full brunt of solar radiation. During periods of intense solar flares, the increased radiation levels can pose a significant health risk to astronauts. Accurate space weather forecasts empower space agencies to adjust mission plans or implement additional shielding measures, safeguarding the well-being of astronauts during their spacefaring endeavors.

- Additionally, for high-altitude flights traversing polar regions, space weather forecasts can warn of potential radiation hazards, allowing airlines to reroute flights or implement necessary precautions to minimize crew and passenger exposure.

In conclusion, space weather forecasts hold immense value in our modern world. By enabling us to anticipate the Sun's activity and its potential impacts, these forecasts empower us to safeguard critical infrastructure, ensure the smooth operation of communication networks, and protect human health. As our reliance on technology continues to grow, space weather monitoring and forecasting will become an increasingly vital tool for ensuring a resilient and sustainable future on Earth.

Intentionally left blank

Chapter 5: Benefits of the GOES-U Mission

The GOES-U mission, as the latest addition to the GOES-R Series, promises a significant step in environmental monitoring capabilities. By leveraging its advanced suite of instruments, GOES-U offers a wealth of benefits across various atmospheric, hydrologic, oceanic, climatic, and solar/space weather disciplines. Let's delve deeper into the specific advantages this mission brings:

1. Atmospheric Benefits

The GOES-U mission offers a significant upgrade in atmospheric monitoring capabilities. It will provide:

- *Advanced Imagery and Measurements*: GOES-U captures high-resolution, real-time imagery of Earth's weather systems, enabling meteorologists to track weather patterns more accurately. These detailed observations are crucial for forecasting a wide range of phenomena, including severe storms, hurricanes, and fronts. Furthermore, GOES-U collects various atmospheric measurements, such as temperature, humidity, and wind speed, providing a comprehensive picture of the atmospheric state.

- ***Real-time Lightning Mapping:*** The Geostationary Lightning Mapper (GLM) onboard GOES-U represents a revolutionary advancement. It's the first operational lightning mapper in geostationary orbit, offering real-time detection of lightning activity across the Western Hemisphere. This information is invaluable for severe weather forecasting, as lightning often precedes the development of tornadoes, hail storms, and damaging winds. By identifying areas of lightning activity, forecasters can issue timely warnings and enable communities to take necessary precautions.

- ***Enhanced Fog Detection and Monitoring***: Fog events can significantly disrupt transportation and pose safety hazards. GOES-U, with its high-resolution imaging capabilities, offers significant advantages in fog detection and monitoring. It can capture real-time imagery of fog cover, allowing forecasters to track fog development and predict its clearing time. This enhanced monitoring empowers authorities to issue advisories and implement measures to mitigate the risks associated with fog events.

2. Hydrologic Benefits

The GOES-U mission extends its reach beyond the atmosphere, offering significant benefits in the realm of hydrology – the study of water on, above, and below Earth's surface. By monitoring various hydrological parameters, GOES-U empowers us to gain a deeper understanding of the water cycle and anticipate potential water-related hazards.

- Precipitation Monitoring: GOES-U plays a crucial role in monitoring precipitation events across the Western Hemisphere. The satellite's advanced imaging capabilities allow for the detection and characterization of precipitation, including rainfall, snowfall, and ice accumulation. This information is invaluable for hydrologists, who can use it to assess potential flooding risks, track the movement of storm systems, and estimate water availability in various regions. Furthermore, GOES-U data can be used for drought monitoring, identifying areas experiencing water scarcity and enabling authorities to implement water conservation measures.

- Snowpack Monitoring: Snowpack, the layer of snow accumulated on the ground, plays a critical role in freshwater reserves. GOES-U, with its high-resolution imagery, can monitor snowpack extent and depth across vast mountainous regions.

This information is crucial for water resource management, as melting snowpack contributes significantly to river flows and reservoir levels. By monitoring snowpack changes, authorities can anticipate potential water shortages during dry seasons and implement necessary water management strategies.

- ***Soil Moisture Analysis***: Soil moisture content is a vital indicator of drought conditions and potential wildfires. While directly measuring soil moisture from space remains a challenge, GOES-U data can provide valuable insights. By analyzing satellite imagery and vegetation health indices, scientists can infer soil moisture conditions and identify areas experiencing drought stress. This information empowers authorities to implement drought mitigation measures and potentially predict the risk of wildfires in drought-stricken regions.

3. Oceanic Benefits

Our planet's vast oceans play a critical role in regulating climate and supporting marine ecosystems. The GOES-U mission offers a valuable perspective on this dynamic realm, providing crucial oceanic benefits.

- Sea Surface Temperature Monitoring: GOES-U plays a vital role in monitoring sea surface temperature (SST) across the Western Hemisphere. SST variations can significantly influence weather patterns, ocean currents, and marine ecosystems. By providing high-resolution, real-time data on SST, GOES-U empowers meteorologists to improve the accuracy of weather forecasts, particularly for hurricane development. Furthermore, scientists can utilize SST data to track and monitor ocean currents, which play a crucial role in global heat transport and climate regulation.

- Marine Heatwave Detection and Tracking: The Earth's oceans are not immune to climate change, and rising global temperatures can lead to the formation of marine heatwaves. These extended periods of abnormally warm ocean temperatures can have devastating consequences for marine ecosystems, disrupting coral reefs, impacting fish populations, and triggering harmful algal blooms. GOES-U, with its continuous SST monitoring capabilities, allows scientists to detect and track the development of marine heatwaves. This information empowers authorities to implement measures to protect vulnerable marine life and mitigate the ecological disruptions caused by these events.

- Fisheries Management Support: Healthy oceans are vital for sustainable fisheries. GOES-U data, particularly information on SST and chlorophyll concentration derived from satellite imagery, can contribute to improved fisheries management practices. By understanding the spatial distribution of chlorophyll, a proxy for phytoplankton abundance, which forms the base of the marine food web, fisheries managers can identify areas with high fish population density. Furthermore, SST data can be used to predict the migration patterns of certain fish species, enabling fishermen to optimize their fishing operations and ensure the long-term sustainability of fish stocks.

4. Climatic Benefits

The GOES-U mission transcends immediate weather forecasting, offering invaluable benefits for understanding and monitoring long-term climate trends. By providing continuous, long-term observations of various climatic parameters, GOES-U empowers scientists to track climate change, assess its impacts, and develop strategies for mitigation and adaptation.

- Long-Term Data Collection: Climate change is a slow-moving phenomenon, and its detection and

characterization require long-term, consistent data collection. GOES-U, as part of the GOES-R Series, builds upon a rich legacy of environmental observations. The continuous data stream from GOES-U allows scientists to track changes in crucial climatic parameters like temperature, precipitation patterns, and cloud cover over extended periods. This long-term perspective is essential for differentiating natural climate variability from the fingerprints of human-induced climate change.

- ***Essential Climate Variable (ECV) Monitoring***: The GOES-U mission contributes significantly to the monitoring of Essential Climate Variables (ECVs). These ECVs represent a suite of physical, chemical, and biological variables that collectively define the state of Earth's climate system. GOES-U data, including information on cloud cover, sea surface temperature, and precipitation, contributes to multiple ECVs. By monitoring these ECVs, scientists gain a comprehensive understanding of the Earth's climate system and how it's responding to external forcing factors like greenhouse gas emissions.

- ***Climate Change Impact Assessment***: The data collected by GOES-U not only helps us understand climate change itself but also empowers us to assess its impacts on various environmental systems. For instance, by monitoring changes in snowpack and precipitation patterns, scientists can evaluate the potential impacts of climate change on water resources in different regions. Similarly, information on sea surface temperature variations can be used to assess the vulnerability of coastal ecosystems to rising sea levels and ocean acidification. This knowledge is crucial for developing adaptation strategies and mitigating the negative consequences of climate change.

5. Solar and Space Data Benefits

The Sun, our life-giving star, can also unleash powerful outbursts that disrupt technology and endanger astronauts. The GOES-U mission, with its suite of sophisticated instruments, offers vital solar and space weather benefits.

- *Real-time Solar Monitoring*: GOES-U hosts a suite of instruments dedicated to monitoring the Sun's activity in real-time. The Solar Ultraviolet Imager (SUVI) and Extreme Ultraviolet and X-ray Irradiance Sensors (EXIS) provide continuous imagery and data on solar flares, coronal holes, and other solar phenomena. This information is crucial for forecasting geomagnetic storms, which can disrupt power grids, communication systems, and satellite operations. With timely warnings from GOES-U data, authorities can take necessary precautions to mitigate the impacts of geomagnetic storms and safeguard critical infrastructure.

- Coronal Mass Ejection (CME) Detection and Characterization: CMEs are massive eruptions of solar plasma and magnetic fields that can hurtle towards Earth, triggering geomagnetic storms. GOES-U, with its Compact Coronagraph-1 (CCOR-1) instrument, plays a vital role in detecting and characterizing CMEs. CCOR-1 images the Sun's corona, allowing scientists to identify CMEs early on and estimate their potential impact on Earth's magnetosphere. This advanced warning empowers authorities to take proactive measures to protect critical infrastructure and ensure astronaut safety during space missions.

- Space Weather Event Monitoring: Beyond CMEs, GOES-U monitors various aspects of space weather. The Space Environment In-Situ Suite (SEISS) and Magnetometer work in hand to measure energetic particles and magnetic field variations in near-Earth space. By analyzing this data, scientists can track the arrival and intensity of solar wind particles and predict their potential impact on Earth's auroras,

communication systems, and satellite operations. This comprehensive monitoring empowers us to understand and respond effectively to the ever-changing nature of space weather.

Chapter 6: Legacy of GOES-U

Building Upon a Strong Foundation of Past Missions

The GOES-U mission isn't an isolated endeavor; it represents the culmination of decades of experience and innovation in the field of weather satellites. Launched as the final chapter of the GOES-R Series, GOES-U builds upon a strong foundation established by its predecessors.

1. A Legacy of Continuous Data Collection: The GOES program, initiated in the 1970s, has played a pivotal role in revolutionizing weather forecasting. These geostationary satellites, positioned in a constant orbit above the equator, provide continuous observations of Earth's weather systems. This real-time data stream has been instrumental in improving weather forecast accuracy, enabling meteorologists to track and predict weather patterns with ever-increasing precision. GOES-U, as the latest addition to this lineage, carries forward this legacy of continuous data collection, ensuring the uninterrupted flow of vital information for weather forecasting and environmental monitoring.

2. Severe Storm Tracking and Early Warning Systems: One of the most significant contributions of the GOES program lies in its ability to track and predict severe weather events. By monitoring atmospheric conditions and identifying signatures associated with thunderstorms, hurricanes, and tornadoes, GOES satellites have empowered authorities to issue timely warnings, enabling communities to prepare and mitigate the potential devastation caused by these storms. GOES-U, with its advanced suite of instruments like the Geostationary Lightning Mapper (GLM), further enhances this capability, providing even earlier and more accurate warnings of severe weather threats.

3. Meteorological Research and Climate Monitoring: Beyond immediate weather forecasting, GOES data has played a crucial role in advancing meteorological research and climate monitoring. The long-term, consistent observations provided by these satellites have empowered scientists to study atmospheric processes, understand climate variability, and track the evolving trends associated with global climate change. GOES-U, as part of this long-term data record, contributes to a comprehensive understanding of Earth's climate system, providing valuable insights for climate modeling and future climate projections.

A Stepping Stone for Future Advancements in Weather and Environmental Observation

The GOES-U mission, while marking the conclusion of the GOES-R Series, also serves as a stepping stone for future advancements in weather and environmental observation. The lessons learned, technologies developed, and data collected during the GOES-R era will undoubtedly pave the way for the next generation of weather satellites.

1. A Bridge to the Future: Geostationary Extended Observations (GeoXO): Looking ahead, NOAA, in collaboration with NASA, is already setting its sights on the next frontier – the Geostationary Extended Observations (GeoXO) mission. GeoXO represents the next evolutionary leap in geostationary weather observation, promising even more advanced capabilities than the GOES-R Series. The knowledge and experience gained from developing, launching, and operating the GOES-U satellite will be invaluable in shaping the design and functionalities of GeoXO.

2. *Enhanced Capabilities for a More Comprehensive View*: GeoXO promises to build upon the success of the GOES-R Series by offering significant advancements in observation capabilities. These next-generation satellites will boast improved resolution, enabling them to capture even finer details of weather patterns and environmental phenomena. Furthermore, GeoXO will likely incorporate additional instruments, expanding the range of data collected beyond what GOES-U currently offers. This comprehensive data stream will empower meteorologists and environmental scientists to gain a deeper understanding of the complex interactions within Earth's atmosphere and climate system.

3. *A Collaborative Endeavor for Global Benefit*: The GOES-U mission, and its successor GeoXO, represent a testament to the power of international collaboration. The development and operation of these sophisticated satellites involve the combined expertise of various government agencies, research institutions, and private companies.

Conclusion

The GOES-U mission, as the crowning achievement of the GOES-R Series, represents a turning point in our ability to monitor and understand the dynamic forces that shape Earth's weather and environment. This sophisticated satellite isn't merely a technological marvel; it embodies the culmination of decades of innovation and unwavering dedication within the GOES program. GOES-U builds upon the strong foundation established by its predecessors, ensuring the uninterrupted flow of critical data for a multitude of purposes.

Beyond the immediate benefits of improved weather forecasting and severe storm warnings, the GOES-U mission holds immense value for the future. The vast amount of data collected by GOES-U instruments will serve as an invaluable resource for scientific research for years to come. This data will empower meteorologists to refine climate models, gain a deeper understanding of long-term climate trends, and anticipate the potential impacts of climate change. Furthermore, the lessons learned from developing, launching, and operating GOES-U will undoubtedly contribute to the success of future weather observation missions.

The GOES-U mission serves as a bridge to the future, paving the way for the next generation of geostationary satellites – the Geostationary Extended Observations (GeoXO) mission. GeoXO promises to build upon the success of GOES-U, offering even more advanced capabilities and a wider range of observations. The knowledge gained from GOES-U will be instrumental in shaping the design and functionalities of GeoXO, ultimately leading to a more comprehensive understanding of Earth's complex climate system.

The data collected by GOES-U, coupled with the technological advancements it fostered, will continue to influence the field of weather and environmental science for years to come. This mission empowers us, not only to prepare for the immediate challenges posed by weather events but also to gain a deeper understanding of the intricate dance between Earth's atmosphere and climate, ultimately shaping a more sustainable future for generations to come.

9 7 9 8 3 2 1 8 3 3 7 5 9